C
811
BEASLEY

Beasley, Bruce
      Summer Mystagogia

DATE DUE

Gilpin County Public Library
Box 551 15131 Hwy 119
Black Hawk, CO 80422

DEMCO

The Colorado Prize

SUMMER MYSTAGOGIA

Poems by
Bruce Beasley

Winner of the Colorado Prize
Selected by Charles Wright

Center for Literary Publishing/University Press of Colorado

Acknowledgments

I would like to express appreciation to the editors of the following journals, in which some of these poems originally appeared:

America: Good Friday, 1993

Antaeus: Ultrasound

Field: By Bread Alone; Primavera; Red Reed; Daily Antique; Witness

Ontario Review: The Monologue of the Signified; First Reading of Genesis

Prairie Schooner: Leper's Lily

Prism International: Doctrine for the Cessation of Misery; Prayer

Seneca Review: The Shadow Wall

Shenandoah: Sweet Repeaters

The Southern Review: Figure; On Easter

Virginia Quarterly Review: Ugly Ohio; The Edges of Things (as "After Words"); Before Thanksgiving

I want to thank the National Endowment for the Arts, The Artist Trust, and Western Washington University for grants that helped in the writing of these poems. And thanks to Tim Lui, Dan Tobin, Robin Hemley, and Bill Wenthe for their support and close reading.

for Suzanne

...ask the living things that move in the waters, which tarry on the land, which fly in the air; ask the souls that are hidden, the bodies that are perceptive; the visible things which must be governed, the invisible things that govern—ask these things and they will answer you, Yes, see we are lovely. Their loveliness is their confession. And all these lovely but mutable things, who has made them but Beauty immutable??

—Augustine

Joys impregnate, sorrows bring forth.

—Blake

Table of Contents

IV.

V.

I.

Idaho Compline

West, and west, the seeable world
urges, and you're drawn
there too, deviable: quarter-
lit over the half-snag
ponderosa pine, then

glinting under the silt
loam and shale, inside
fire-scarred root-wads
ripped out
of eroded hills...

I have to squint
hard to find you
in the dusk shoving the visible lake
back to its far cove;
I have to squint hard
to witness
anything *but* you
in what dwindles and flames nearby,

in the forest
understory, where all
is infestation, and fight:
crumble of humus,
worm and moss, cancerroot
and skullcap, dwarf
mistletoe deforming the firs
into a gnarl of witches' broom,
unhealable limb—

Where the dogtoothed
violets and yellowbells
decompose their colors into night,
I glimpse you
rising off the burnt end
of Lost Man Trail, blear

as the drift of mist
into the gulch under Cougar Mountain,
where I can't
reassemble you, running
my finger through woodpecker drills,
over loose, bug-ridden bark
on the blackening hemlock and larch.

There's nothing I want you
to give me:
I've quit asking
for anything but desire—
windflower and anemone in the nurselog's
woodrot,

syringa and white spirea
overgrowing the boarded-up passage
into an abandoned mine.
Everything's gotten out,

Lord,
constellations
dropped like waterstriders on the lake—

Whatever's to be divined

won't be tonight:
the child I've wanted
won't show its face,
won't tell me how it's withheld;

my father and mother, gone
twenty years, recede
deeper into my forgetting,
where they only
speak in the garble of dream...

What's to come
migrates in its own time, unhinted-at,
self-divesting

         —as you divest
yourself again of all my goings-on,
even the words on the tongue,
the eye as it scans
the blacked-out lake
of Coeur d'Alene

looking for some sign of signlessness,

someway to belong , for a moment,
to the fugitive
ripeness of whatever is.

Orphic

How sensuous
to close the eyes

and seal everything
in that splotched

dark: coppiced
mulberry trunk, red

poppies in fissures of pumice,
furred bark of the sweet chestnut—

Nothing vanishes
when I look at it there,

though I turn
inward and gaze for days...

Psalms of grieving, thanksgiving,
bring

back everything I've seen:
olive tree

bent to take in the lightning,
Eurydice's

shadow over mine, pale on black
on the cracked

tufa, before I walked back alone.

Ultrasound

The Loneliness One dare not sound—
—Dickinson

1.
Halloween, and we flew
toward my grandfather's deathbed
in Briarwood Convalescent, in Atlanta,
while the ticket agents, in holiday
skeleton suits, giggled.

That morning, after the phone call, the Puget Sound
rose and spat in its mist
behind the traintracks and smokestacks
of Georgia Pacific, as Suzanne and I
walked by the seawall (she bearing
for eight weeks a child he'd never see now),
watching the rain reswelling the Sound,
the water reverting to its first, shapeless
form—

And no one could read the ultrasound
pictures two days later,
after his funeral on the Day of the Dead,
after the casket
scraping its metal cradle:
through a swarm of static,
three black, interlocked
circles under a mass of cyst—
twins, the doctor guessed, or *triplets*
or *molar pregnancy*: the fetuses
feeding as triple tumors on the uterine wall—

I'll tell you what I'm not *seeing*,
a doctor said,
I'm not seeing any heartbeats.

2.
In our minds we filled them in
as they would have been:
with their arms—the pregnancy book said—only as long as
exclamation points,
with their lung buds and their tongues,
already-beating hearts
migrating into the sealing flesh of their chests,
with their bodies weighing less than a thirtieth of an ounce,
we imagined them taking hold,
primitive, physical, quickening, ours.

3.
In the newspaper that week, a photograph
of the vicinity of a black hole:
like the ultrasound pictures, three swirls of black,

in an X of caught dust:
                                inescapable
turning-inward, decreation
of matter and light.
It hides at the center of the galaxy,
and nothing comes back from there.

4.

Nothing which exists, says Simone Weil,
is absolutely worthy of love;
we must therefore love that which does not exist.

Decreated ones,

you who turn back from matter,
from the Sound held on the horizon
by the freeway and a coiled black smudge of mountain clouds,

you who reveal yourselves
as empty
black marks on the photo strip, the dumb
hum of life-machines,

you, my grandfather, who
shouted, stripped to your diapers, near the end,
I'm in the middle of something,
but I don't know what I'm in the middle of,

I'll stay here, in the middle,
in the fifteen-hour nights before the solstice,
in the season of a sacred birth,
where the apple tree bears up its three weak leaves,
where you of ninety years, and you of nine weeks, vanish,
and the earth goes on bearing
too much
that isn't you:
always excess, and always
this helpless wanting more—

          —wanting to witness
a voice, above words, beyond sound,
that would read
this strip of loss, these
pictures of what isn't there,

and sound for me the washed, gray
gash of the harbor,
the black sacs in static haze,
the mudblack trench of my grandfather's grave,
and fill in for a moment

whatever is gone,
the Sound always lost in cold, blown fog.

II.

Figure

I.

In the garden, tufts of purple toadflax.
An earth the mind couldn't know
what to make of, so
palpable it was,
so taken in by the senses.

In the beginning, nothing could be made.
Not mind
but matter

appeared to matter...

Therefore, a restlessness: a
scratching under things

till at last the mind broke
through into sound,
as if language
could replicate or outdo
the evidence of the ears:

the birdsong trying to redeem,
through sheer repetition, its lack of meaning

till vowels oozed
from the human mouth, trying
to voice what the tanager voiced, except
with sense

and in time
a lightning-cleaved birch
came to mean
not wood and wormhole and split, waterlogged bough

but a figure
for dividedness, a story
about polarity
and interdependence, twins—

enemies—whose lives converged
when they found themselves
in love with the same woman,

whose name was Death,

while the thing itself—the riven tree—
stood barely acknowledged in its woodenness.
The myth
didn't know how to include
the sweet
burnt odor of moss-draped
flaps of bark...

II.

Today, on Sehome Hill, a burn
on my fist becomes transfigured
into *a sting of nettles*:
language of the mind, no longer
even recognized by the stung hand.

But that's what it takes
to stake our claim here.
This wouldn't be our world
if language
didn't violate every fullness,
make a lack
for the mind to invent

in—
woodpecker's bug-ridden cavity in the branch—

and give us days
rich or deprived
with metaphor and myth,
a world more embrangled than the body
insists it is,

as iris and tympanum and tongue
repeat again and again
(whether or not we believe them)

their true, disfigured tales.

Primavera

She would have starved me out of the underworld
if she could have. He fed me
seeds that glistened red, he said
I needed at least that much
sustenance, reminder of earth. I needed
nothing but the hard realm of his body:
his ribs cold against my breast,
my tongue on the bones of his shoulders.
Now, dredged back, I can feel
blighted crops stir with an urge
to sprout. And I hate
this power of hers
over food and sex
she's forced on me, hate
being like her: sunflowers
droop and poppies wrinkle at my touch.
He's down there, watching, I know,
he must think
I belong to her inbreeding land again.
So I love to rake the fertile earth
to a compost of worms and beetles, rustle
the corn till I find a smear of slugs
on the stalks.
Just to spite her. And then feel the decayed
things burrow underneath, to the deeper
parts, where they belong,
and me. Above, stunted
tufts of olive trees; iris
and lobelia, and bullocks
straining their yokes through the deep
seed-rows; I straggle
through harrowed fields, remembering
how once the ground
unclosed for me. Now
my mother, in black veils still,
wails over crocus and rose. She watches me
close as I walk from bush to bush,

suspicious,
afraid I'm not even the girl
she ravaged the crops to get back.
I think she longs for a new excuse
for her ritual mourning, the power
withheld nourishment
gave her. And in the starved,
bare flats of Hades, Dis
moves like her shadow, rousing
his own envious grief.
He can't stand not touching me
and he gazes through the furrows
as I squeeze the orange blooms
in my fist, spit,
tear the spears of hyacinth as quick
as she makes me
make them bloom, and fill
—just for him—my mudstained
apron to overflowing
with withering stalks of lilies.

By Bread Alone

1.

I scraped
the last scraps of white
from the crust
and laid them on my sister's tongue,
while crows marked our father's
black road home.

2.

She was starving; everything was.
Horizon specked with ravens swooping
around a house in the hemlocks
that glistened with clumps of sugar, a dark
candy chimney they swarmed but left untouched.

3.

Food, and fire: duck-fat
sizzling on the coals. Vats
of chocolate spattered
the baked walls. The old woman
spooned it into our mouths, greedy

to be loved. And fed us
everything we looked at:
honeyballs and chestnut torte,
windowseals, the sugared frame of a mirror.

Gretel told her how
the oaks had shivered from our father's
axestrokes
before he left us in the woods
with only a day's worth of bread,

and how even that I'd scattered in the mud.

4.

After days of gorging
we began to call her Mama. She made us tell
how our father chugged his rum with trembling hands,
so drunk he'd choke on his soup. She swore
she'd never leave us
hungry, never
let us go. Rubies
glistened sharp and tight around her throat.

5.

Gretel never wanted
to stop eating.
She begged Mama to keep the oven full
and they kneaded
together all day as Mama
whispered stories about a little girl
with a father too weak to keep her alive,
a stepmother who hoarded the few
scraps of sweets for herself,

and a brother who'd rather feed the birds than her.

6.

They were always together. Gretel
barely spoke to me anymore
except when she came to my room
to feed me slabs of crumb-cake.

I slept all day, dreamed
of blood-stained axes, children
picking red berries
out of blackbirds' mouths.

7.

Gretel said there was nothing
worth remembering, nothing
to be afraid of anymore. Mama
nodded behind her, gaunt,

the kitchen
nauseous
with its odor of marzipan
still cooking, rum-cakes
gone stale.

8.
The loaved ceilings began to crack
from the oven's heat, and burnt
sugar oozed in black
streaks along the walls.

Mama asked me why
I'd grown so quiet, why
the ladyfingers lay
untouched around my bed.

9.
Gretel was scared all over again,
I could tell:

scared I wasn't fat enough.
She begged me to eat
the lumps of fried dough, Mama was
furious over the waste,
she said, the useless
weakness.

10.
One night I woke from a nightmare,
and ate

a square from the roof above my bed
and another, and another, till a branch

of hemlock broke through
and I could see the moon again, and smell

wet leaves of the black forest
and a putrid curl of smoke

from the chimney's dough.
The moonlight shone a path between the trees.

11.

Gretel wouldn't go.
She said she'd never let me

bully her back into those twisted woods,
never go anywhere near the old shack

with our drunk father, the scraps
of bread and muddy gruel.

She said I was jealous that Mama
loved her more than I knew how, gave her

everything a girl could ever need.

12.

All that was years ago. I live alone now
in the deep hollows of a hemlock

somewhere near my starving parents' house.
I never even found out if they survived.

13.

But when I hunt by day, the trails
have a way of leading me back

to the stale
house of sweets, half-eaten,

where my twin sister stares through the window,
dark eyes sunk in her bony skin, hungering

for the next lost child,
clutching his belly, to make

his way through the forest and taste
the burning ginger of the broken house.

First Reading of Genesis

The clipped
nubs of rose-stems scratched
the picture window
where a black
Bible was propped open
on the sill. Still
stiff in mt Sunday school clothes,
I couldn't stop
staring at one sentence
from Genesis:
It repented the Lord
that He had made man on the Earth,
and it grieved Him at His heart.

I'd just learned to read
well enough
to take in the morbid story:
the woman made out of a rib,
the snake who could talk, the murdered
brother, and six chapters in
God already hated everything he'd loved,
it grieved Him at His heart.

Till the rain
came, and came, and came...

The floor furnace clanked and spat its burnt air

while my father
cussed in his bathroom,
rattled the medicine cabinet.
I could tell
from the scratch of ice against whiskey-glass
the bottle was almost empty,
and the liquor stores closed till Monday.
I knew even then how to read

the signs, and when to pretend
I wasn't there, and stare
at the rain-fogged window,
rubbing clear circles the size of my face
then watching them shrink to a point,
wiped out by one breath.

On the porch, an empty begonia pot
dribbled mud from its cracked side.

Come out of that witch's coven
or I'll break your neck:
my father's voice.
And my mother's:
Go to hell, Harold, you're drunk.

The rain beat and beat but it couldn't touch me.
I stood over the slatted furnace,
letting that heat
singe my shoes, rise
to the roots of my hair.
All afternoon, rain slashing the window,
the sirens repeating their one sound,
I made believe
Goddamn you   my father's
slurred, anonymous curse

wasn't meant for me.

A Mythic History of Alcoholism

Narcissus

After work every day, Daddy
would stir his drinks over the sink,
stare for an hour
into the bathroom mirror,
watching himself get drunk
enough to come out for supper.

Vesta at the Hearth

Bacon-hiss, spatter of fat:
Mama steadies her hands to hoist
a half-gallon jog
of vodka
to her mouth, throat
pulsing with gulp after gulp
then she sneaks it to its hiding place
behind the crock pot,
smushes biscuit dough under her shaking palms.

Denial: From My Diary, Age 10

"Woke up.
Ate breakfast.
Went to school.
Came home.
Raked yard.
Jumped on pogo stick.
Made fire in back yard
and roasted hot dogs.
Daddy was drunk.
He kept hitting Mama.
Watched TV.
Went to bed."

From My Dream Diary, Age 10

"We were primitive people.
Daddy had to hunt for our food.
When he gave me fish eggs
to eat, snakes
kept hatching out of them."

Silent Night

The year I quit talking to my father,
he saw Jesus
under the Christmas tree,
crouching, tense, accusing—
He woke me at midnight
and insisted I sing.
Silent night, holy night,
All is calm, all is bright—
The furniture around us was smashed,
the mirror splintered on the wall—

Inferno

This region
of Hell is constructed
from the brains
of the damned, stitched

one to another, still
conscious, eternally
despairing,

my dream-
guide tells me, *Look,*

this one—viscid,
pinkish-gray, throbbing—

is your father's...

Psyche, in Bed with Knife and Lamp

I couldn't sleep, listening
to the clatter of whiskey glasses
on the night tables,
my parents' garbled voices
over Johnny Carson's,

*one blow of this hammer
and you'll be gone,*

and I lay stiff,
my heartbeat hard against the sheets.

The Sacrifice of Isaac

The woodcutter's axe
thumping far away, somehow
comforting,

Hansel
hunched in the dead leaves,
calling *Father...*

But he found
only a branch tied to a withered tree,
banging in the wind.

When he got home:
*Wicked children,
why did you sleep so long in the forest?*

Denial

Everything will be
allright again
if only the moon lights

Hansel's
trail of stones. The cottage
lamps will be burning late;

Father and Mother, through the windows,
blowing

so tenderly to cool the steaming soup.

Adoration of the Magi

Star of wonder, star of light—strobe
of police car's red and green
over iced pavement, and the three

strangers at the door: then
Daddy in the squad car, in handcuffs,
Mama pleading

Let him go, everything's
fine now, though
his head is bleeding from the gash
where she'd fought him back with a high-heeled shoe...

Then my brother and I riding our new
ten-speeds through the sleet,
trailing scraps

of silver wrapping paper,
Mama waving from the door
Merry Christmas boys Do they ride OK?

Watching Mama for Signs of
Drinking After Daddy Died

Forty nights without rain:
Noah walked the mountain, stepping
suspicious on still-spongy ground, watching
doves drop twigs from their mouths,
gash of rainbow across the half-dark sky.

The Serpent Beguiled Me

I can't live with your daddy
unless I have a little
something to drink,

Mama said, smiling, neck
splotched with bruises, pouring
them both another whiskey.

After he died: *I can't*
live without your daddy, clutching
her fifth of vodka
as she stood

over the hissing iron, crying—

Leaving Childhood

It never stays far enough away.
An accidental
click of the ruby slippers, and everything
grays and grains into Kansas

again, the blown-away house
restored, pitchfork

43

still stabbed in the dirt,

and everyplace
I turn looks, uncannily,
like home...

Elegy: Narcissus and Echo

Narcissus is drowned, and Echo

helpless not to repeat
his last words: *O darling boy
whose love was my undoing;*

helpless
not to repeat
chugged liquor, delirium tremens,
the locked
psychiatric ward,

then the grave plot

by the Ocmulgee.
Twice in five years, I walked there,

in black, watching
the world stir, dulled,
distorted on the river's brown skin—

Alas, Narcissus sighed, bending
to drink from that longed-for image,

that perfect self the drinking could never reach,

and Echo, in pity, was able
to answer
with her own voice, her own
wasting-away
after him, *Alas*.

Philomela and Penelope, Weaving

The story's never told, the tapestry

where the knife's raised
to the tongue
unravels before it's finished,

memory
taking back everything it gives,

its voices
murmuring *Everything's*
fine now, or
self-accusing: *Why*
did you sleep
so long in the forest,

a thousand and one
more nights, on each
a tale
untold, threads

fraying even as they tighten.

Humpty Dumpty

Isis is reassembling Osiris again:
her papyrus boat
poling through the marshes
because the putting-back-together is never done—
So: map the bottle's daily
changing hiding place:
trashcan, fireplace, cookie jar, commode.
Pour out what's left of the whiskey
when they're passed out and the liquor stores are closed.
Record your father's

rages, leave the tape
on the kitchen table at breakfast.
Tell your neighbors
he's only gathering firewood
when he stalks the yard
with a hatchet, Mama
locked hiding in the car. Beg
the police to come
one more time. Fall
silent for two years.
Dream you're cutting his throat.
Blame yourself,
if it makes you feel better. Isis
is gathering from the reeds of the Nile
a basket, an arm, a tongue. The reassembly's
always going on: hold
together the cracked
mask of myth, its
pieces sharp and useless over your face.

Irresistible Grace

Quince bloomed, and fruited, rotted, and bloomed again;
moon whole and red, then yellow and mostly gone—

Eve and Adam walked the mudflats, downcast,
eyes locked on the sealed horizon.
Their footprints and their shadows in the mud. The river's
always pushing-forward
repelled them:
where did it have to go?
The still swamppools held their image more precisely.

They lay
together in the cragged riverbed,
faces in the silt-full downwash, mossed
driftwood like weapons in their hands.

*

The exorbitant
ordinary would have to give up its fullness:
olive and pomegranate, swollen
branches of Knowledge and Life,
serpents humped together, dull-eyed, in the sun.

From the beginning, His order
was fixed, inscrutable.
The creation had nothing to regret,
and therefore held its stasis.

*

Endless duplication of bloom.
Pacing the stream's whole length
—siltbank and shoal—
they learned fullness

meant containment:
against the sun, a gate of fruit trees;
away from sun, a barrier
of flowering stone.

He who breathed them out of muck
would hardly speak,
refused them even His name.

*

All His dullness, self-
satisfaction,
He had to violate again, to end
the restless rest He couldn't shake.

To Eve, at His command, the serpent spoke:
Can you imagine what hunger
tastes like,
its savor on the tongue?

And already grace
moved, glimmering,
the way barnacles hold a surfspume
a moment after the tide is gone.

*

Everything needed to be burdened
by longing, by something to need,
but deprivation

still waited for its moment of creation . . .

Take this, and eat, he said.

How could things
have been otherwise, with grace

so compressed, and finding
in the whole garden no outlet?

*

Sated, they sought what places
He had neglected to keep filled:
husk of locust, hollow driftlog sunk in weed.

Together they named these
God-missing.

Their prayer:
Maker of flesh,
withholder,
grant us, too, what you had always,
until now, enjoyed—
the void, the universe without you.

*

He never hurt
them: clawed footprints,
serpents' slither-tracks through the mud.
They wanted something to hurt them.

Refused garden: marred
until they could want it,
until it seemed unambiguously theirs,

whose mistake was it, whose greed.
Out of whose pain does the Maker stir.

III.

Witness

1.

That's where your father
had his accident, my father
mumbled, pointing

through the cracked windshield
to the dropoff where he'd plunged that car
into dead shrubs thirty feet below.

But I knew
from my mother's enraged voice
on the phone, then from the barred

psychiatric ward, it was no
accident;
he'd never said a word about it before.

That gesture—his finger tracing
vaguely all he couldn't talk about—
comes back to me now, through

Caravaggio, where Christ
guides the apostle's pointing finger
with sexual tenderness

into the smooth, apparently permanent
gash in his breast.
Through his one sentence, my father's

voice was rough with such regret—
for having tried, or having failed,
I couldn't tell—

I only knew his scarred
arm on the steering wheel
scared me, and his sweet

whiskey breath, and the broken guardrail
stabbing its twisted metal
over the skidmarks still there down the edge . . .

I thought: he must have tried to make it stop.
But I didn't want to know,
didn't want to watch

his headlights scoop out that canyon
or the darkness fill it back up,
or his lips, lit by a cigarette stub,

try to tell me what had gone wrong
and I didn't say a thing
as he twisted the radio dial

from gospel to Muzak to static,
coughed his dry, frightened cough,
and watched me from the side of his eye.

The torn seat squeaking on its hinges
was the only sound as we rumbled
down the brick streets of Macon,

where I watched his back
disappear through glass
doors throbbing with dancing bottles.

                    2.
In Caravaggio's painting, the voyeur
apostles throng
so close around Jesus and Thomas,

gazing hard as the fingertip
slips into the dollop of wound.
They all want to know what its like

inside the cut, risen body,
but they're scared of what
the touch might do; it's assuring to watch

the curious one
penetrate first. But Thomas
is tense, hie forehead ridged,

his throat tight as he goes
deeper into the fresh
blood just under the skin—

he's mortified, like one
admitted where he can never belong.
Still, Caravaggio has torn

the shoulder seam
on his red robe, which means
he's as human as Christ,

available to damage too. My father
died a year after that ride, and now
I don't even know

where the road he showed me
is. At fourteen, I closed my eyes,
and let his old Nova

carry me home,
the Ocmulgee River's
smell of mud-clogged kudzu and swampgrass

washing over my father's Jack Daniels.
He turns back to me now,
when I want him to, lifts

his shaking hand to the window,
and points again down the cliff,
and the flesh-

colored robe opens, and the finger
pierces just under the heart,
and the hand with its nailhole coaxes

the bewildered witness in.

Good Friday 1993

Yet dare I almost be glad I do not see
That spectacle of too much weight for me.
—Donne, "Good Friday
1613: Riding Westward"

I turn my face
to the purple blooms of bleeding heart
around the porch, then to the one
tern flapping west
toward the harbor's cusp,
riding headwinds against the coming squall.
Nothing here this morning seems much worth
your rage or even your indifference.
At the New Age church down the block
("A Today God for Today People")
no one walks the stations of the cross,
or kneels to kiss its lacquered fir. It's comfortable
to watch the east, there's not much there,
where the Cascades
are gone in the usual clouds,
and the Top of the Tower
revolves its cocktail bar.
The day feels endless: committee
meetings, laundry, H&R Block at 3.
You look toward me,
if you look at all,
with ennui and loathing, and I don't blame you.
Toward dawn, I walk the city's westward bend,
where Squalicum Harbor's sailboats banged their hulls,
and a crimelight hung above the Shrimp Shack's door.
I watched the west
go from dark to dim enough to trace
the seagulls' angry scavenging,
until that light clicked out, and I could stand
to see the sun I hadn't even wanted
rise into its own caul of black
cloud as the Cheerful Little Cafe

unclanked its metal cage.
Now schoolkids, loosed by holiday,
stab umbrellas at a yapping dog
through the fence's
broken slat. Over the poplar's rising
waver like candlefire, the blue
gloom of the east heads toward me
down Victor, and a siren goes
off, and off, and off, on Utter Street.

On Easter

I lop the cherry's rotted, lichen-covered limbs
all morning until Mass,
sawing the moldering wood
through a dim shadow of white stem-clusters,
hacking the scissor-shaped split
of a hollowed fork till it wrenches
loose in my hands, and shivers
a scurf of blooms
from a living branch; crack
of sawdust-spilling wood, white larvae
slick on the underbark
that's scrolled, mottled, and tough
like shed snakeskin—
I don't even know why I bother, now
that the whole tree's in flower:
it must be vain, so late in the season,
to rip from the trunk the rutted wood
that squanders the sap,
to chop it down to bearing limbs
that within a month might forge what fruit
they can, if at last what's dead gives way.

Prayer

Pink light on wet snow, the low
neon glaze of the west
where the skyhigh sign
resumes its place, its one
word obscured by halflit sawmill smoke—

I used to name the names of your sorrows,
but when I wrote them, they grew pale,
indefinite, ink slurred by snow.
You who know them so well, tell me again.

The Monologue of the Signified

*When the present does not present itself, we
signify, we go through the detour of signs.*
—Jacques Derrida

What dwells in the letters of *dwelling*?
Or in your starved syllable *I*,

so restless, so isolate, straining
upward so hard it wards
away the words on either side
with its limbs.

It hurts me
to speak like you, in these
rent syllables, always
scrambling from one crumbling word to the next—

What is meant

is meant to disintegrate;
with every scrape of consonant against vowel,

I empty myself, and you squander me.

                    *

Even now you're not hearing me, are you,

when I tell you
what it's like to be mute...

I can speak
in a way you can't even imagine,
monoglossia
far above all the anger of language.
But for you there are only these words—
cowering, badly

camouflaged:
how they stagger
when I snatch them.

*

Do these labials
and repetitions
please you:
lobelia
bulimia,
landspit spar? Vocables
are a form of starvation: it's no use
pretending you'd survive without me
in a life
so nourished by *meaning.*
Your little verbs, when I abandon them,
are ravaged,

their ribs stabbing through.

*

Somewhere someone is trying to tell you
something language can't house;

somewhere someone is trying to give you
a living less barren than the one
you crush and crush out of nouns.

Why can't you stop naming long enough to listen;
when will you hoard up your treasures,
foolish ones, in me?

*

Names aren't numinous,
only the named is.
So the idea of God

founders in language,
where it's always belonged.

Stripped of what's sacred, you hanker
for what you dream I could give you
if you brought me
your twenty-six-thousand words
to fill:

Here's what I've done with them.
I want
what thrums through the cords
of your throats
to utter *me* whole, want
to inhabit your vulgate:
glottis and tongue.

I keep
coming down to you
so pitifully, waving
the half-masted flag
of your words:

Is this really
all you think
you can get from me,
strangers:
plink
of nickels in your beggar's cup?

The Reliquary Book

Peacocks in onyx and mother-of-pearl,

Golgotha's
sponge of the Lord

molded in gilded
silver: the binding's

ornamentation—all
along its spine tiny

bone-chips
from the 10,000 Virgins of Cologne—

In the museum, it's propped
under glass, splendid

in sun-shaft: RELIQUARY
IN THE FORM

OF A BOOK... And inside,
secreted,

the inaccessible
treasure: thumb-bone

or Cross-splinter, chalice's
shard, no one

will crack it to discover
what's saved

there. The volume's
shut up and dazzling

with unturnable
pages, its

passages
unmovably bound—

Still, this
transubstantiation,

the inside
emerging: the book

broken
out all around its gristled cover

with lurid stigmata of corals.

IV.

Before Thanksgiving

Abundant deprivation,
glossolalia
of hail on windows, the splintered
ice-crust of the roadside muck:

I take names
of things that remain—
stinkhorn rising over dead sweet basil,
the roses' chokehold, still, on the frozen summerhouse.

Doctrine for the Cessation of Misery

I don't know if the Buddha was right, if life

is suffering,
or whether, if all appetite for things
were spent,
I'd lie easy

along this lawn studded
with hundreds of cracked acorns, mangled
moles cats dragged from their tunnels—

I don't know if the October morning sun
would touch me then without touching
anything,
or the damp cool of its wind
press onward toward another more
vulnerable perceiver—

But I know there's a weariness
dulling me: throb
of blood through the temples,
squeak and scrape of mockingbird cry,
train's rattling jangle behind the creek.

I sit in a porch swing and feel nothing
but languor
for language and hunger,
hundreds of pages blurred meaningless by my eyes.

It's dispossession

I want:
bucket's scrape on the dry well's floor,
the tedium
of sentences suffered no more—

This morning in exhaustion I lay down
The Roots of Lyric,
and realize I know nothing
of this seed
before me,
still cupped in its broken shell:
what germinates
when the acorn decays at last,
what purpose
all this seedfulness
could serve.

The oak
stirs its shadows over the shingles,
rattles loose
one acorn drilled with a perfect, tiny hole
I stare into and see nothing,
then crack under my heel
to expose only shallows,
a grainy black sludge...

I don't know if the Buddha was right, if all things
are on fire
with weariness, love, and lamentation;
I only know appearances
suffer
my depletion,
as the skin of the cracked acorn
can't be
separated from the rough,
striated wood of the shell;

I see only mingled
appetite
and suppression: tempered sunlight,
loose lid of cloud.

Wind
riffles pages of *The Roots of Lyric*:

the chapters—Chant,
Charm, Riddle,
Emblem,
     Ideogram—
accuse me of disaffection,

the wonder of being dulled
to a life
so lured into words.

The Edges of Things

Always language
on the edges of *things*,
parasitic, hungry
for meaning—

How I want it: *mourn*
and *extinguish*,
exoskeleton
and *wing*...

I murmur
"Lent" means spring, murmur
cracked rocks on the creekbank, slimy
with moss,

and whisper
in incantation:
ammonia,
amnesia, memoria,
          Medusa...

—What a sweet
heap it falls into: mash
and windfall, rot

and ferment.

Red Reed

Nothing exists except atoms and emptines
—Democritu

Look within
these words to the rough,
yellowing grain of the page
that herds them on all sides, and drives
hard in-between each letter:
sinkhole of the u, the locked
cavity in the head of each e...

Everything insubstantial—

Like words, atoms
are mostly empty:
the nucleus
the proportion of an apple
in a baseball field, with the rest
of the stadium
all but vacant...

Look beyond the page to your hand,
so limp, so powerless there,
a hooked birthmark, maybe, under the thumb,
or a wedding ring wedged in the heat-swollen flesh—

And again, beyond words, to the room,
say a white string
hanging beside a bare 60-watt bulb,
or a day sliced by venetian blinds
into dogwood and cracked porch column, pink
woodwasps nagging at the peeled white paint.

It keeps
growing particular: what this
ink would have you witness—

Mayday and mayfly, catalpa,
folded beach umbrellas
lined, like gravemarkers, by the sea.

Look down at this page, look hard,
until you can notice
nothing
but your own gaze,
and give up what that gaze can't reach:
the pale green lines on this white pad
in Ohio, in 1992, in May,
the sweetgum's green through the window,

or whatever image of green
you recall as you read this
and forget
as you do
the pounding under your ribs,
the insuck of air
that keeps drying the rough grain of your tongue—

or the reddish
reeds on a creek bank, here,
now, through this window, the ones
you read, homonyms, or real
reeds, thick-rooted in mud, that swarm
greenflies the moment you part them—

Ugly Ohio

I know what we call it
Most of the time.
But I have my own song for it
And sometimes, even today,
I call it beauty.
—James Wright,
"Beautiful Ohio"

I don't know why I live in Ohio,
where Stinking Creek
slithers past Hot Dog Heaven, and snowmelt
polishes the mashed, colorless weeds,
and locomotives
hunker past the beds of wasted orchards,
and the splintered windows of the Funeral Home.

Ice-stubs in mud, swaddle of mulch:
half-hearted unfreezing, Plum Creek's
skin of ice
salving its cuts
with its own melt—

April first, still the scab of the year.

                    *

All I want
is to believe
in what pleasure
a flawed world can give,

in what sunlight
is doing to the wrinkled crusts
of oakleaves
that lasted all winter;

76

to thrill in the whipped
flag over Tappan Square
slapping its fifty stars,
in the quick sticks of the dead azaleas.

But I'm restless for Georgia's
figs and Cherokee roses, the pale pink
acid juice of the pomegranate,
tangle of lilac and lavender, and sweetgums
scalded to their roots in drench-rain and lightning.

                    *

CLEAN DIRT
WANTED, says a wet, scribbled sign
in a pasture by the dead-end highway,
strict rows of shadow and snow
laid like a plough's furrows.
I've never known *what* the bloated silos hold.

I could tell you
it's beautiful, this half-frozen muck,
the stench of mudslides in sewer-bilge,
the burnt-yellow factory smoke
over cowbarns,
but it would be, like the refuge of smalltalk,
a way of holding what's ugly at bay—
only a metaphor, and a lie,
metaphor meaning "To bear change."
And nothing changes,
not even in April, in the flat,
streaked streets
of my alien Ohio,
except the white crumble
of last fall's
petrified dogturds
suddenly under my feet in Orchard Street's thaw.

Sweet Repeaters

> *What part of a gambler's long-buried*
> *childhood is it that forces its way to*
> *repetition in his obsession for play?*
> —Freud

In the hypnagogic
casino, I lean
to the clitter
of dice on the green
felt of the numbered table,
shoulder to shoulder with the loud
crowd crying

All the hard ways,
while the shooter
spits in his fist,
bone-
rattle of die against die.
The stickwoman,
whose nametag says VENUS,

resumes her always-changing
chant, as the dealers
haul in the lost bets:
Undershot,
Short by a dot,
Nothing sweeter
Than a repeater...

There's something
soothing in the patterned
repetition—hard
four and easy six and snakeeyes two,
even
in the seven's rough
enchantment,

78

its power to wipe you out
or make you new.
It's not money that matters
but the measured
order, the hard
way through the fracas
on the table's

deranged and garish yellow and red—
then the pleasure
of reversion, the coming-again
of my number before the deadly 7,
when the bet pays off its two for one...
Then there's harmony again, and I go back
to where that order

started, to the first
cadenced world where I held
number-shaped plastic blocks
in my fist (how sinuous
the six; how jagged, even then, the seven)
as I memorized
their names and shapes, the spells

an x or + could make them
cast.
Now the dice
trapped jerking in my palm
like a grasshopper,
now the rune of their rolling
over the Babel of $5 chips,

over painted dice on the felt
and the 4
forces its way to repetition
in the hypnagogic casino
and the red
stacks of chips, lit
by the roulette's distant neon wheel

double again,
and the Nooksack's
craps table hollers again, the shooter
having found at last his measure.

V.

The Shadow Wall

You are a shadow and a shadow you see...
—Dante, *Purgatorio* XXII

That hurlyburly of Virtual
World: on the science museum's
basketball court, dribblers

swipe at empty air, leap
to rimshots only they
can see. Children

in goggles hang-
glide deep
through their minds,

squealing, while a TV screen
shows us where they think
they swoop: rims

of skyscrapers, gulches,
and petrified trunks
they veer between.

We turn to the real, the naked
mole rats' glass tunnels,
read the plaque

about how—cold-blooded, fanged,
underground—the queen
and her chosen male

cripple
or kill any others
who try to breed...

Infertility's
on our minds: artificial

insemination, Clomid,
motility and progression
of sperm, the body
our bodies refuse

to make. All around us,
rejections of flesh, the urge
to be only a brain and its

attendant signals:
at the virtual woodlathe
(its invisible

splinters and sparks
in the eyes) a father
waits for his child to emerge

to the sensible world again.
You can understand
how much love scalds me,

Dante's Statius says, when I
forget our emptiness,
treating shades as solid things...

He kneels to kiss
Virgil's ghostly feet.
I try not to believe

there's a spirit-child,
invisible, evading us,
afraid of being *marred*,

as Plato says the soul is,
*by communion with the body
and other*

miseries...
When I need

to remember our emptiness, I come

and watch the naked mole-rats, all
grotesque, inbred
physicality, huddles

in their tunnels, gnawing
each other's necks—
or slip into the cave. . . room

of the Shadow Wall, and throw
my body against the padding
in a blaze of artificial

light, stand back and watch my own
shade linger, contorted,
trapped

in the shadow-holding
phosphorescence
a few moments

after I'm gone, surviving
my body
as if it were solid

flesh, as if
it could last,
even if it were.

Summer Mystagogia

mystagogia: the period immediately
following the initiation into a
mystery

...to discover an order as of
A season, to discover summer and know it...
—Wallace Stevens

I.

4th of July: fireworks over Squalicum Harbor
hiss and vanish in a mist
strung down from the mountains.
The aquamarine
and viridian trails of fire
fizzle out in a muffle of cloud;
only their last sparks
rip through, cut under,
while the white
we'd ordinarily ignore
is revealed as itself, shocked

open, lit for a moment from within.

II.

Transfigurations of summer, the used
knowings of things
worn down: I stare
hard at this Thursday afternoon,
trying to make it surrender
whatever spirit underlies
its drought and incessant bloom:
quick shadow of gull
over surf-dreck, suck
of clamhole at low tide; in
the dilapidated boathouse
scribbled with *Life shits* and *Jesus
is Word made flesh* and
Suck me off,
I stand over and outside it all,
watching.
But no prayer burns the day into order,
nothing makes sense of the sensuous:
only tidewash again, and sundown, and gulls
snapping scraps of meat from burnt campfire sticks.

III.

The profligate
scum of wave, the hundred
crows in one poplar—
47 million sperm
on the fertility doctor's microscope slide,

his language *hysterosalpingogram,*
intrauterine insemination,
an aggrsseive month for the ova,

and, watching white globes
of cottonwood seed
glide through stabs of sun and fall
all over the mossed rock at my feet,

I think of Jesus' parable
about the seed that died on rocky ground.

Tell me
why seedpods are pouring
through a forest
that has not a single ungreen spot to fill.

IV.

All day the Sound casts back its mess
of seal-head and seaweed-strangled driftlog,
over stained, split rocks crushing morning glories.
All the relentless
materiality of summer—
seagulls lined wing to wing
all along the tanker bridge.
Too much
of the brine-smell, the sugar-ooze of fruit,
too much the world
made up
by the senses,

so disorganized, so resistant
to order...

V.

I used to live in a house without order.
I used to live

in a house without rooms,
organized around a vodka bottle

none of us could find.
It was the foundation, the rock center,

and everything we did
we did in response to it:

hidden deep in a clothes hamper, or
in a box of Kotex where my mother

thought we'd be ashamed to look,
it built the disordered house around itself,

arranged and rearranged
its own unchanged significance...

Look at your mother, she's drunk,
my father

laughed, Mama slumped in the bathtub,
she doesn't even know who you are...

VI.

A weakening of the sense of reality—
that's what a mystic called sorrow,

saying joy is what we know when we know the world
for what it is. I know

a black litter of sea-pearl rose petals
in mud, under a dandelion's

half-blown stem...
There are days, like these, when faith

erodes a little, baring the root.
And empty stakes in the garden mark

what's lost when the blooms are gone—
Hungry

for structure, for things that don't change,
how can I live in this house

built on the sands, the neaptide creaking below me?

VII.

No wonder tonight
the weeping silver birch
whips its fronds as though trying
to dislodge,
onto the narcissus and scarlet bleeding hearts,
all the dusklight it's hoarded.
No wonder the past seems
impregnable, and the moment of passage
into unambiguous dark
is deferred, twilight troubling its borders.
No wonder the world looks like

a place without wonder.

VIII.

I live in a house that's stood for a hundred years
under a path in the sky where Arctic terns
shrill inland an hour after the ten o'clock dusk,
where gulls chase an eagle from the harbor down Voctir Street.
I live in a house
built on the grounds of a syphilis clinic
so the doctor could escape his patients' cries—

On Sunday nights, the wind
(always on Sunday, no one can tell me why)
ravages this house,
once tore a door down the middle
and slung it across the yard.

In the sandy garden, salmon-colored poppies
drag over lavender and lambs' ears.
Three slugs crawl across dogshit
that weights the petals.

Deep in August, the hollyhocks'
hundred blooms drag their stems to the ground.
A scraggle of yellowed tomato vine
offers up the one ripe,
distended fruit
that kills it...

And morning glory forces its way
through cracked floorboards
into the house.

I stand at the window, listening
in the scrape and crush of wind
for the orders

I can barely make out anymore

of some magnitude, some
transfiguring spirit
I need:

all
the muck and mystery
of summer, how
can I enter it?

The Meantime

For a time, and times, and half a time...
—Revelation 12:14

1.
For a time, and times, and half a time,
I wait
for something to charge the days, electrify
chronology—
But the summer only washes from flood to drought,
poison ivy twining the gate doors.
Between the twin
cherry trees, constellations
knot like vines:
the Hunter's sword, horn of the bull,
all nebulous to me, inscrutable. In my fever
a faceless one
hands me the Book of Revelation:
a honeycomb scrawled with hieroglyphs. I turn
and turn its chambered hollows in my hand.

2.
This is the meantime: interruptions
of thundersqualls over thickets of fireflies,

swamp-smelling
July twilights, cicada-sizzle along the nerves—

Unredeemed
progression, sequence without end...

But at night I lie in a bogland
where I have buried what's left of my soul—

the brown and shriveled casing of a seed—
in the cold mash of peat, and wait

for it to flower again over the slough,
so I can harvest its fruit, return

my ripened spirit to my body:
But all summer the dream ends the same way,

with a summoning
shriek of waterbirds,

and a pomegranate
blighted at the blossom-end, blackened

seeds dried inside
the torn, decaying rind...

3.
Slag time,
weeks not worthy of memory: it's hardly worth
marking
the slather of sap, crackle of dead beetles. Time
without intervention, now
after now—

Shrill of the porchswing, the mockingbird's
insistent, repetitive reply:
like everything they're instantly
displaced
and elegized by memory, like each night's
vanished intensity of dream: leaving
and re-entering the meantime.

4.
Counter-linearity of the sea:
how the waves
efface themselves in withdrawing, leaving
rivulets, dreck
surging backward in the foam—

Their message

is repetition, not
arrival: continual
culmination, eschaton
without end:
the dream's
purple neon signboard
flaring *Sea
Gull, Sea Gall, See
Gall,*
before the beach's foul,
acidic spume—

5.
The fullness of time

and its rot:
purple drip from the glut of grapevines
staining the crabgrass,
the chaotic order of wasps swarming stem-clumps of souring
fruit,
everything swollen and jammed by heat—

Then sundown, the horizon
bound shut, its low
sun in a split sheath of clouds—

The last things
are already unveiled,
available, if only I see them
here where I bide the time:
in the thick gnats in dim floodlight,
in heat-lightning haze
over rasping
stalks of corn, the rutted weedbed, compost
crush:
in moments of suspended
shock, August

as climacteric, first sessions of the end—

Daily Antique

Already it's enough, the passage
out of now and into now

transfigured,
last flash of windborne

leaf in Halloween's first dark:
not long ago now was the Fourth of July,

firecrackers' whistle and scatter-
rattle over the Sound,

summer settled in umber slouch along the hills.
And the roadside display, ANTIQUE

TABLES MADE DAILY:
the grained

lacquer flashing as our headlights passed.
Already it seems too much, the morning

paper we couldn't find last month
snagged high in lilac limbs still, its headlines

as useless as the early
leafrot under globed streetlights,

Freddy Kreuger
four-year-olds

escorted up the drive. Haunted
end of October: All

Souls, All Hallows,
Day of the Dead, clocks

wrenched back an hour. Everything

stirring that should be gone. Restless

transition, synapse, though one
now resembles the next

so wholly it's hard to find your way
among them. Mirror-hall:

everywhere you turn you surprise
yourself, turning

and surprised. I write
what I can, while *then*

fattens itself, *not-yet*
fasts and dwindles, dwindles and fasts,

yellow words
shoving black space

down the screen, blinking
cursor marking the *now*

that recedes before you
like the raft in a dream

and here
we are, water-

treaders thrashing in the swell.

Leper's Lily

1.
It's later than it's ever been before,

and now it's even later. Now the past
swells to take the delphinium and iris

I'm watching through this wet-on-wind—
I smell the rain before I feel it—

on which the seagulls draw their arcane figures.
And memory will get rid of most of it.

And memory salvages a crumb
of another summer: pits of bitten cherries

dropping all around me as crows
and jays and mockingbirds

swarmed, all at once, the fifty-foot tree.
Fullness, and loss: the doctrine of plenitude

says God created everything there could be,
that could be good. Piece by piece it vanishes

in time, and reappears when memory
hauls in its nets, heaped,

glimmering, smelling of decay.

2.
The storytellers
always agree on one point: looking back is fatal.

So Eurydice
dwindles into mystery, and Demeter

wastes the ground with a grief she can't let go.
Whatever love we've left behind, whatever Sodom

we turn back to in longing,
is like the breadcrumbs Hansel and Gretel

watched vanish in the breaks of winter birds.
Back there, the oven's always stoked,

the torn heart fat on its stick.
When the prodigal son returns

to the calf fattened in the field,
his dutiful brother, forgotten, begins

his own dejected wandering, and no one misses him.
Still, I like to watch

how hungrily the forgotten
shores itself on memory, leaving

behind its corrosive layers of salt—

3.
What is it, Plato wants to know,
that's always becoming,

and never is?
Right now the story around me becomes

that same thing it was, and will be,
stagnant Sunday, memory backs and fills

with loss what isn't changing. Grace fills,
says Simone Weil, the empty spaces,

the voids that grace itself has carved
to fill. I never really understood what she meant

until I saw, in the Butchart Gardens,
the leper's lily:

its hanging blooms
named for the warning bells on lepers' necks.

That the given world mixes
beauty and mutilation

the Gnostic knew, and had a name for it:
hiemarmene—the delusive

attraction of the beautiful
that lures us to satisfaction,

flies' murmur in the web. I name it
grace, the world given us

to perish in, to lose and hoard,
the wrinkled skin of the just-bloomed

orange poppy
ours to watch, and reconstruct

in memory two weeks later when it's closed
in on itself, grotesque,

the leper's lily swinging its bell,
as we become

what all our losses make us,
sipping

in bare winter
the pomegranate's bitter juice.